Copyright DT FUTURES INC PUBLISHING. All

This book is copyright protected and intend
may not amend, distribute, sell, use, quote,
content within this book without the full cor
company, and/or copyright owner. Making copies of these pages or any
portion for any purpose other than your personal use is a violation of United
States copyright laws.

Disclaimer

DT Futures Inc Publishing and its authors have used their best efforts in preparing these pages and their publications. DT Futures Inc Publishing and its authors make no warranty of any kind, expressed or implied, with regard to the information supplied.

Limits of Liability

DT Futures Publishing and its authors shall not be liable in the event of incidental or consequential damages in connection with, or arising out of, the providing of the information offered here.

Want Free Ebooks Every Week?

Receive free ebooks delivered directly to your inbox! We promote our eBooks FREE for the first 5 days of every publication. That means you will be the first to know when new books are published. Out collection encompasses a wide variety of topics.

Visit www.FreeEBookClub.com

Contents

Grilled vegetable

Egyptian Rice Recipe

Spicy Egyptian Dukkah With Chickpea Flour

Basila wa Roz

Turley (Mixed vegetables and meat)

Egyptian Falafel Recipe

Egyptian Feta Cheese Spread

Feteer Meshaltet Recipe "Arabic Pie

Revolution Koshari

Lemon-Mastic Mehalabia Brûlée

Egyptian Hummus

Egyptian Stuffed Veggies

Maklouba

Egyptian Rawani cake

Egyptian Style Beef Liver

Egyptian Kofta

Ethiopian Ful Medames – Fava Beans with Berbere

Grilled Vegetable

INGREDIENTS:

1 zucchini
1 squash
1 eggplant
1 red pepper
1 green pepper
oil
3 cloves garlic, crushed
1 tablespoon vinegar
1 can cut tomatoes Mexican style
1 c. water
2 jalapeño pepper cut thinly sliced
salt, pepper
1/2 teaspoon basil

1/2 teaspoon thyme
1/2 teaspoon oregano
1 onion cut into 8 wedges
1can beans
2 tomatoes sliced

PREPARATION:

First, preheat broiler to 250 C.

Second, cut zucchini, squash and eggplant around 1/2 inches thick.

Third, in a planning sheet brush all vegetables with oil and sprinkle with salt put under stove fire cook likewise, fire sear for around 10 min. till vegetables are seared not busted.

Fourth, chill off and remove the skin from the pepper and cut into cuts in a pot warm 1 tablespoon oil, incorporate garlic and sauté for around 1 minute, add vinegar warmth to the point of bubbling

Fifth, include tomato sauce, water, jalapeño, salt, pepper, basil, thyme, oregano cook on medium for 5 min.

Sixth, organize vegetables and onion in a heating dish spread with beans include the tomatoes sauce and layer crisp tomatoes. Heat it at 350 degrees for 40 min. Cool and serve i

Egyptian Rice Recipe

INGREDIENTS:

1 c. dry vermicelli

1 tbsp. olive oil

1 c. long rice

1/2 c. onion, chopped

2 ¼ c. boiling chicken stock

PREPARATION:

First, break the vermicelli into pieces.

Second, in a skillet, cook the onion in the oil until it is translucent, and transfer from pan.

Third, cook the vermicelli pieces in leftover oil until it is golden. Then add onions back to pan and add rice; mix it to combine. Pour it in boiling stock, mix.

Fourth, cook it over low heat for 20 min and serve it.

Spicy Egyptian Dukkah With Chickpea Flour

INGREDIENTS:

½ c. chickpea flour

¼ c. lightly toasted unsalted peanuts

2 tsp. coriander seeds

2 tsp. caraway seeds

2 tsp. lightly toasted dill seeds

1 tbsp. lightly toasted sesame seeds

½ tsp. kosher salt or coarse sea salt

½ tsp. cayenne pepper

2 tsp. sumac

PREPARATION:

First, in a frying pan over medium-high heat, toast the chickpea flour, stirring constantly until it begins to smell toasty and darken slightly. Transfer immediately to a bowl. Then, chop the peanuts and add to the bowl with the chickpea flour.

Second, heat the coriander seeds, caraway seeds, dill seeds and sesame seeds in a skillet over medium-high heat, shaking the pan until each is fragrant and beginning to smell toasty. Transfer from the pan and let it to cool.

Third, working in bunches, consolidate the coriander seeds, caraway seeds and dill seeds in a zest plant and toil to a powder. Exchange to a dish and blend in the sesame seeds, salt, cayenne and sumac.

Basila wa Roz

INGREDIENTS:

1 onion

1 tablespoon of organic olive oil

2 tablespoon organic butter

3 c. of organic peas

1 can of organic tomato paste

1 1/2 c. of water

1/8 teaspoon sea salt

1/8 to 1/4 teaspoon organic cayenne pepper

2/3 teaspoon of cumin

1/2 teaspoon of organic thyme

2/3 teaspoon organic garlic powder

PREPARATION:

First, put 2 tablespoon butter in a frying pan on medium heat. Dice onion and cook it till light brown and translucent. Then, add 1 tablespoon of olive oil and peas and cook for 3 min. with ¼ teaspoon of garlic powder and salt.

Second, add the organic tomato paste, water and mix till it becomes a sauce. mix in all seasonings except the lemon. Cook it on low heat for about 10 min.

Rice

1 ¼ c. of organic basmati rice

1 ¾ c. of water

1 tbsp. olive oil

Salt

PREPARATION:

Wash rice well and join water and rice in a pot. Turn warm on high, once the water bubbles diminish warmth to stew and spread with a top. The rice takes around 15 min. till cook, blend periodically to keep rice from staying.

Turley (Mixed vegetables and meat)

INGREDIENTS:

1 pound green peas
1 pound green beans
1 pound carrots
1 pound potatoes
2 pounds minced beef
5 c. fresh tomato sauce
1 c. onion, diced
Seasonings (Salt, black pepper, hot chili powder, cinnamon and nutmeg)

For frying: vegetable oil
2 tomatoes, sliced

PREPARATION:

First, wash all vegetables very well

Second, Peel potatoes and carrot skin. Then, cut them in to small cubes.

Third, in a pan put diced onions and meat, on a medium heat cook it till meat turns brown then, add seasonings and mix well then pour tomato sauce and reduce heat. Cook it for 10 min.

Fourth, in a skillet put vegetable oil. Then, fry carrots, potatoes, and other vegetables medium frying
Fifth, in a baking tray, spread a layer of cooked meat then put a layer of vegetables. Keep adding layers of meat and vegetables but let the last layer be meat. put sliced tomato on top.
Bake it for 30 min. in the oven at 180 C.

Egyptian Falafel Recipe

INGREDIENTS:

1 C. white broad beans, dried

1 onion

3 garlic cloves

1 leek stalk

1 tsp. of baking soda

1 tsp. of flour

1 tsp. of cumin

1 tsp. of cayenne pepper

3 tbsp. of sesame seeds

5 sprigs of fresh coriander

5 sprigs of fresh dill

5 sprigs of fresh parsley

½ tbsp. cooking oil

1 tsp. of salt to taste

PREPARATION:

First, soak beans overnight in water

Second, chop the onions, garlic and leek stalk and put it in a mixing bowl. Then, include the leaves of the coriander and parsley to blending dish. At that point, include the flour, preparing pop, cayenne pepper, cumin and salt to the dish.

Third, add the beans to the blending bowl and mix into a green glue. At that point tender kneed. In the event that two sodden include a little flour, if excessively dry include some of water.

Fourth, Heat the oil until it is gurgling. With a wet spoon shape the blend into level circles. Sprinkle softly with sesame seeds and add to the hot oil until it has turned cocoa evacuate it all things considered.

Fifth, serve Falafel with hot pita bread, vegetables salad and hummus.

Egyptian Feta Cheese Spread

INGREDIENTS:

Feta cheese

2 tbsp. olive oil

2 tbsp. lemon juice

3 scallions, chopped

10 cherry tomatoes, chopped

2 tbsp. chopped parsley

To garnish: olive oil and chopped tomatoes

To serve: Pita bread

PREPARATION:

First, combine in a bowl the feta cheese, olive oil, lemon juice, scallions, chopped cherry tomatoes and parsley until creamy.

Second, garnished it with a drizzle of olive oil and chopped tomatoes. Serve it with pita bread.

Feteer Meshaltet Recipe "Arabic Pie

INGREDIENTS:

4¾ c. flour
1 teaspoon salt
2 c. water

PREPARATION:

Preheat the oven to 500 °C.

First, in a mixer, put flour, salt and water and blend until the dough becomes smooth and elastic piece.

Second, Divide the dough into equal parts and press by hand to remove the air. Form into balls and grease with melted butter, put aside for 15 min.

Third, oil pieces with oil and spread the batter pieces on a marble surface and take off with a moving pin until they turn out to be thin.

Fourth, pull from all sides and fold from four heading until you get a square shape. Leave the last piece took off for the base.

Fifth, put the collapsed pieces amidst the base piece. At that point, overlap the four sides toward the center to make a square with alternate pieces inside.

Sixth, bring the corners around the filling to make a circle. Then, place on a tray greased with Oil and Bake it on the oven for 15 min. until golden brown.

Revolution Koshari

INGREDIENTS:

500 gram of spaghetti, cooked al dente
2 onions, chopped
2 tbsp. of ghee
400 grams of cooked chickpeas
150 grams of brown lentils, cooked
For the sauce:
1/3 c. of olive oil
5 tbsp. of tomato paste
2 leveled tbsp. flour
7 cloves of garlic, sliced
1 1/2 tsp. of chili powder
3 tbsp. of vinegar
1 tbsp. of brown sugar
6 cups of water
Salt and pepper, to taste

PREPARATION:

Make the sauce:

First, heat the oil in a pot on medium heat. Then, add the flour and tomato paste. Always speed until consolidated into smooth glue. Cook it on low warmth for 1 min. until it starts to sweat.

Second, add the sliced garlic, chili and vinegar and incorporate into the roux. Then, add the water, mix then boil once and decrease heat to a low simmer. Cook until thick.

Third, Mix the cooked pasta with the chickpeas and lentils and set aside. Fry the chopped onions in the ghee until it become brown color. Serve the sauce over the pasta and garnish with fried onions.

Lemon-Mastic Mehalabia Brûlée

INGREDIENTS:

Lemon-Mastic Mehalabia Brûlée

3 c. of cold full cream milk

3 tbsp. of cornstarch

¾ c. of sugar

½ tsp. of mastic grains

1½ tsp. of freshly grated lemon zest

Extra caster sugar for the brûlée

PREPARATION:

First, break up the sugar and cornstarch wide open to the harshe elements drains and put on low warmth. At that point, include the mastic and lemon pizzazz and blend consistently to consolidate and to avert blazing.

Second, Keep mixing until thickly coats the back of a spoon. Separate into serving bowls and cool in the ice chest for 3 hrs. When you're prepared to serve, sprinkle a liberal, even layer of sugar. Utilize propane light to caramelize the top.

Third, Allow it to rest for a few minutes and then serve.

Egyptian Hummus

INGREDIENTS:

400g Chickpeas, dried

2 Tbsp. of olive oil

2 Tbsp. of Tahini

3 Tbsp. of Lemon Juice

¼ tsp. of Salt

Pinch of Cumin

Pinch of Cayenne Pepper

1 Clove of Garlic

Chopped Parsley

PREPARATION:

First, soak chickpeas for 12 hrs. Drain them and then cover in a pot with cold water and bring to the boil. Cook it slowly over low heat at a temperature of about 180°C for 1 hour. Then drain it and let it cool.

Second, Peel garlic and chop it finely, add the chickpeas, olive oil, tahini, lemon juice and salt into the blender and blend into a fluffy paste. If the hummus looks to dry add a little more oil and lemon.

Third, Put the blend past into a serving bowl, add a pinch of cumin and stir.

Fourth, drizzle olive oil on top as shown in the picture above. Serve it with fresh and warm pita bread.

Egyptian Stuffed Veggies

INGREDIENTS:

1 kg mixed vegetables (like zucchini, green peppers, eggplant)

½ c. coriander leaves

½ c. flat leaf parsley

2 onions

1 hard tomato

2 tbsp. tomato paste

1 tsp. cracked black pepper

¼ tsp. white pepper

Salt

¾ tsp. cumin, crushed lightly

¼ tsp. coriander powder

½ c. oil

1 c. Egyptian rice or

1 tsp. ghee

8 pieces gum Arabic

1 chicken bouillon cube, dissolved

PREPARATION:

First, top and core the insides of veggies.

Second, wash rice and drain it. Chop herbs very small; wash in a sieve and drain. Then, dice the tomato.

Third, mix rice, herbs and tomato. Then, add spices to rice mixture.

Fourth, fill veggies with the rice mixture 3/4 full to allow the rice expand.

Fifth, heat chicken broth cube, ghee and mastikah until the mastikah melts.

Sixth, Layer the veggies in a level pot or preparing tin. At that point, add chicken soup blend to veggies and permit it bubble on the stove top.

Bake it covered at 180°C until veggies are tender

Maklouba

INGREDIENTS:

2 eggplants cut into rounds
1 head cauliflower, cut into florets
1 teaspoon spice mixture (ground cinnamon, ground cloves, ground cardamom, and ground nutmeg)
3 c. Egyptian rice, soaked for about 30 min.
2 tablespoon olive oil
2 onions, sliced
4 c. chicken stock
Salt

Oil for frying

Nuts (cashew and pine nuts), roasted

PREPARATION:

First, season eggplants with salt and allow standing for an hr. Then wash it

Second, fry cauliflower in a frying pan in oil until it is golden brown. Then transfer it to a plate lined with paper towels. And then fry the eggplant rounds.

Third, drain the rice. Then combine the rice and the spices in a large bowl and season it with salt to taste.

Fourth, Coat the base of a round pot with oil. Mastermind 50% of the seared onion rings and 50% of the eggplant adjusts on the base of the pot. At that point, include 33% of the rice blend. Include a layer of the singed cauliflower, then another third of the rice blend on top. Mastermind whatever is left of the onion rings and eggplant adjusts on top of this.
For the last layer, include the last third of the rice blend on top of the onion rings and eggplant. Press marginally. Prick in a few spots with a wooden stick. Pour the stock over this.

Fifth, cover the pot and cook over medium heat until it starts boiling. Reduce heat and let it cook for 30 min. until tender.

Sixth, transfer the pot from the warmth and let rest for 10 min. put a huge serving plate on top of the pot and flip it over. Precisely, lift the pot off the plate to uncover the layered dish. Trim it with simmered nuts and parsley

Seventh, cooked meat or chicken can be added between the layers to increase the nutritious value of the dish.

Egyptian Rawani cake

INGREDIENTS:

¾ c. flour

¾ c. semolina

¾ c granulated sugar.

5 eggs

Pinch of vanilla powder.

For the syrup:

2 c. of granulated sugar

2 c. of water

½ teaspoon of lemon juice

PREPARATION:

First, combine the semolina and flour in a dish and whisk the eggs together and add the vanilla and sugar then mix it well.

Second, Add the semolina mixture and combine well, pour it in a baking dish and bake it for 45 min. in a 180 C in to pre-heated oven.

Third, make the syrup by conveying the water to overflow with the sugar, vanilla and lemon juice, bubble for 5 min. at that point decrease the warmth and stew it for another 20 min.

Fourth, Pour the syrup while it is hot and the cake is additionally hot, trim it with coconut pieces. At that point, cut it in squares and serve.

Egyptian Style Beef Liver

INGREDIENTS:
4 tablespoon olive oil
1 lb. beef liver, chopped in to 1-inch chunks

8 minced cloves garlic
1 onion, chopped

1 chopped bell pepper
2 hot chili peppers, seeded, minced
2 tablespoon ground cumin
1 teaspoon salt
½ teaspoon ground cinnamon
¼ teaspoon ground ginger
¼ teaspoon ground cloves
¼ teaspoon ground cardamom
3 tablespoon lime Juice
1 tablespoon chopped fresh parsley

PREPARATION:

First, cook garlic, onion and peppers in olive oil in a pot over medium heat. When vegetables have softened and onion is translucent, add the liver and all the spices except the lime juice and parsley.

Second, cook until the liver has changed color. Cover, decrease heat to low and cook until liver is tender, about 15 min. stir it once.

Third, when liver is tender, mix in lime juice and parsley to thoroughly combine. Serve it immediately with pita bread or rice for sopping up the savory sauce.

Egyptian Kofta

INGREDIENTS:
1 lb. ground beef
1/4 lb. ground lamb
1/2 c. minced parsley
1 grated small onion
2 minced garlic
1 tablespoon salt
1 teaspoon crushed black pepper
1/2 teaspoon cumin powder
1 teaspoon nutmeg
olive oil Spray
1 piece of coal

PREPARATION:

First, combine the onion and garlic with the spices and let it sit for 15 min. then, add the meat and the parsley to the onion and mix well and shape it into kofta shapes.

Second, splash the base of a huge skillet with the olive oil. Heat the container over medium high warmth. At that point, include the kofta and sauté on all sides. Bring down the warmth and spread the dish. Cook it for 5 min. At that point uncover the dish and let any fluid vanish

Third, when cooking the kofta, get the coal prepared by putting it on a medium high fire until it turns dark. At that point, make a stash that will hold the coal: Take a bit of aluminum foil overlap down the middle then overlay the edges to make the take shape

Fourth, put 1 tablespoon of olive oil and the hot coal to the foil.

Fifth, at the point when the kofta is cooked, exchange it from the warmth. Make a gap amidst the skillet, pushing aside the koftas and put the foil stash in that opening and rapidly cover the dish. The smoke from the coal will fill the dish and implant the koftas.

Serve kofta after 2 min. and garnish it with parsley

Ethiopian Ful Medames – Fava Beans with Berbere

INGREDIENTS:

6 big crusty rolls

¼ c. olive oil

4 cloves garlic

1 c. minced white onion

1 teaspoon berbere

6 c. cooked fool (round fava beans)

Salt

6 tbsp. green onions, sliced

6 tbsp. crumbled feta cheese

1/2 cup finely diced tomato

1 finely diced jalapeno

2 hardboiled eggs, cut into slices

1 tsp. cumin powder

PREPARATION:

First, put the rolls to lightly toast in oven.

Second, put a skillet over medium heat and add the olive oil, and fry the garlic and onion for 2 min. then, add the berbere and cook for 1 min. Then add the ful and 1 c. of water and bring to a simmer.

Third, transfer from the warmth; crush the full, adding water if necessary to achieve the surface of refried beans. Add salt to taste. Come back to the warmth quickly.

Fourth, embellish ful with olive oil, green onions, feta cheddar, tomato and jalapeno. Top it with the egg cuts and sprinkle them with a little cumin powder. Server it with pita bread

Want Free Ebooks Every Week?

Receive free ebooks delivered directly to your inbox! We promote our eBooks FREE for the first 5 days of every publication. That means you will be the first to know when new books are published. Out collection encompasses a wide variety of topics.

Visit www.FreeEBookClub.com

Printed in Great Britain
by Amazon